Crazy Awesome Animal Things Adult Coloring Book

By Alina Bradford

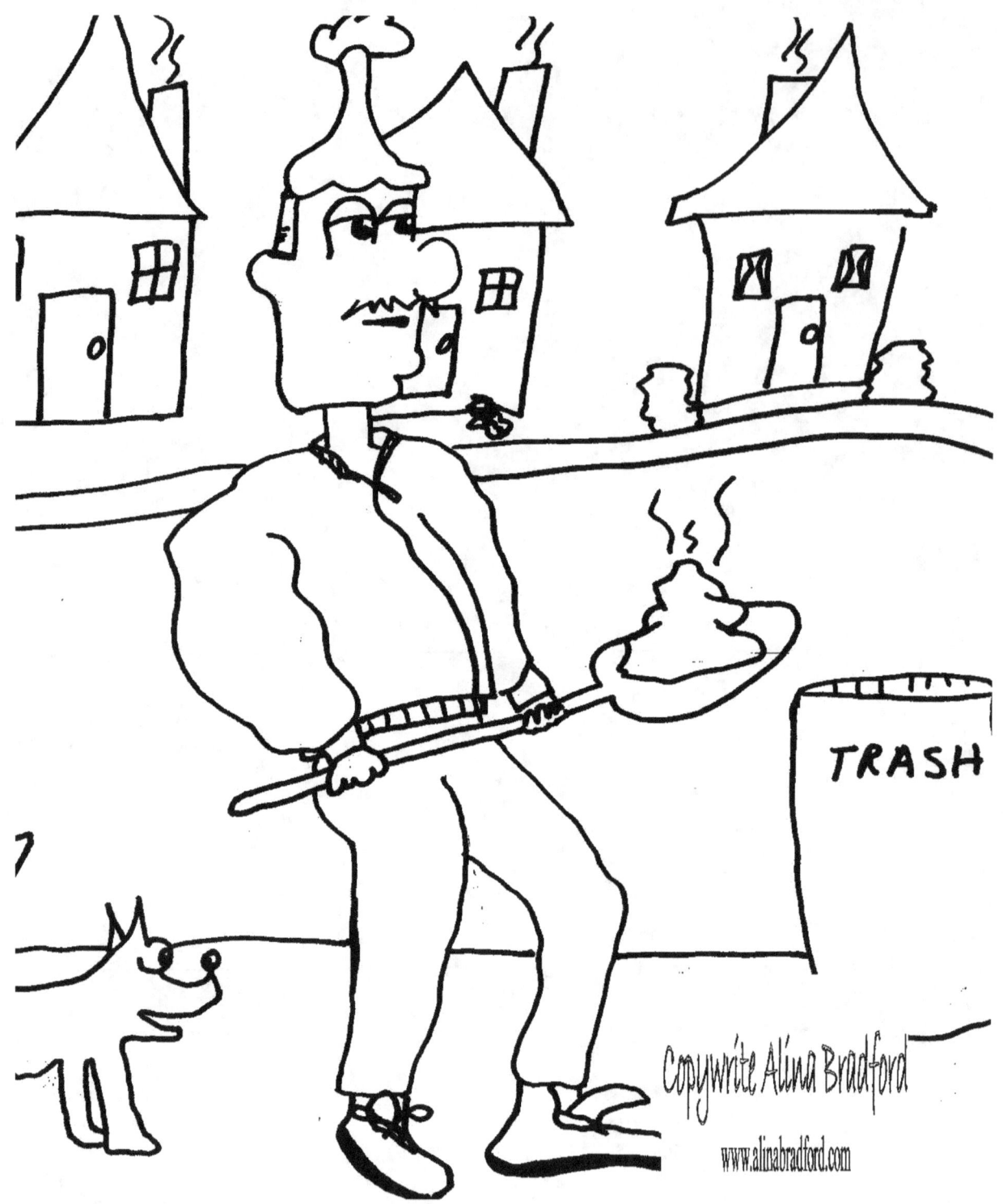

TRASH

This coloring book has several different levels of difficulty throughout. There are crazy complicated zentangle pages for when you are feeling ambitious and simpler pages for when you don't have a lot of time. Each and every page features fantastical animals with attitude.

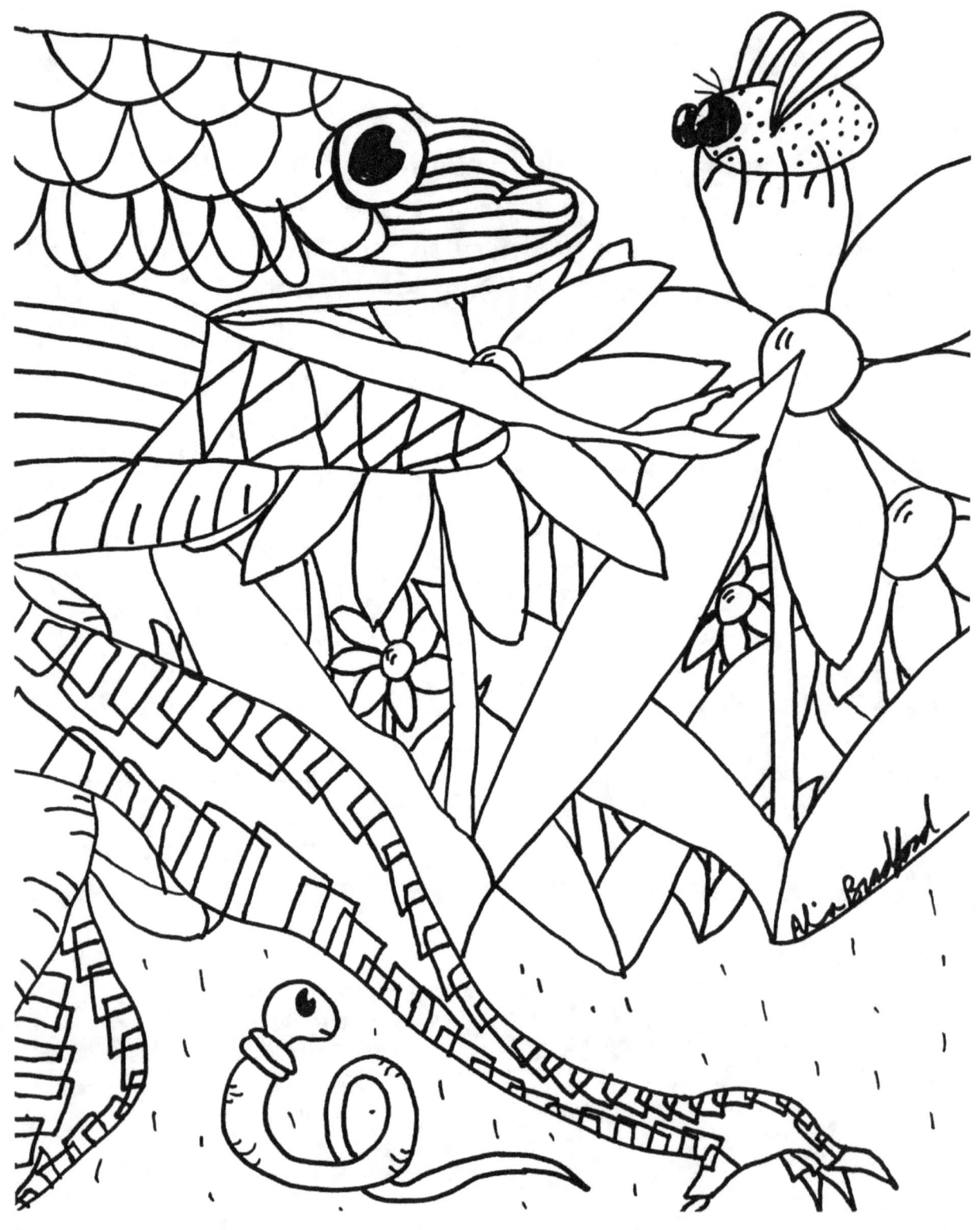

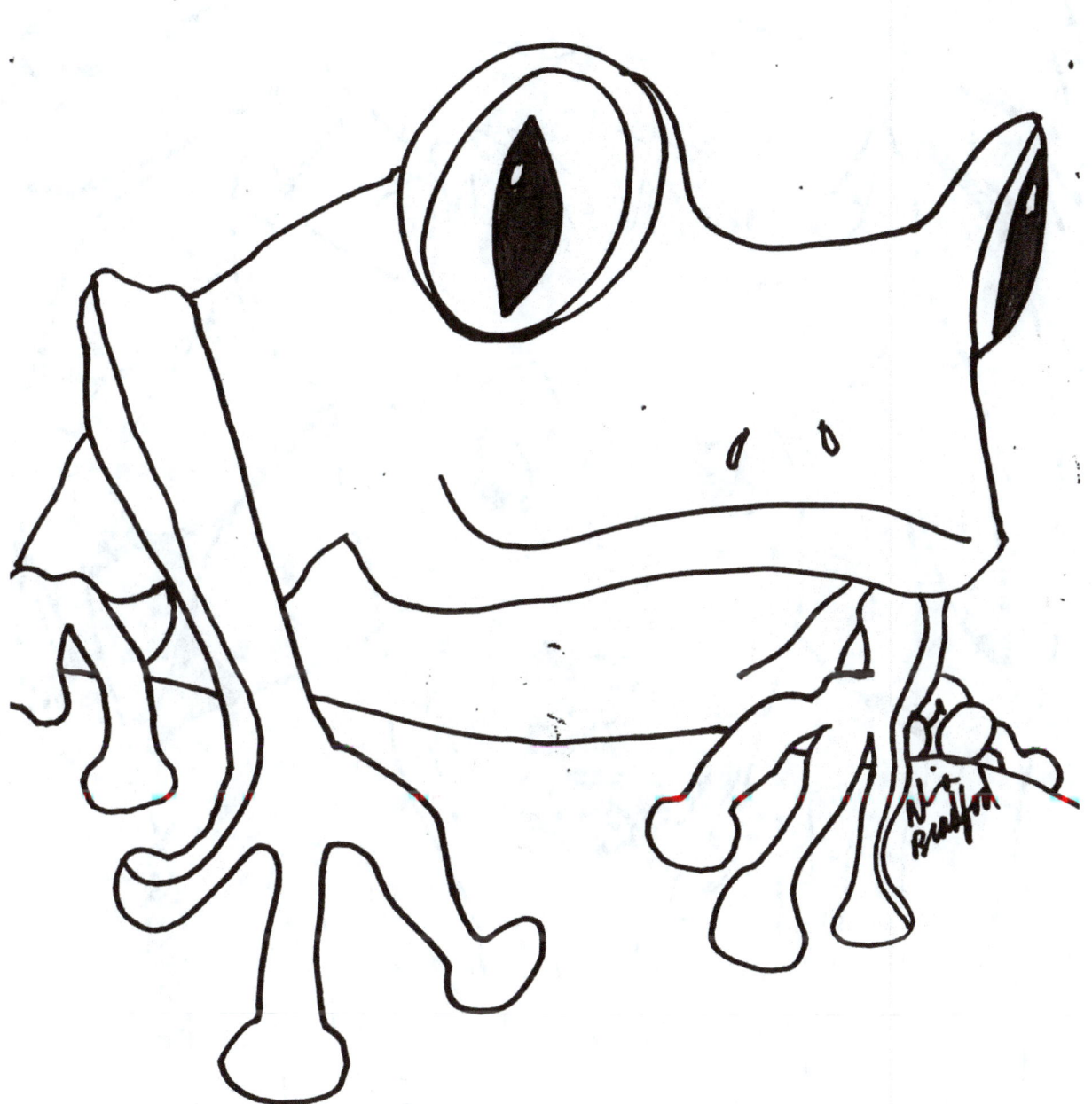

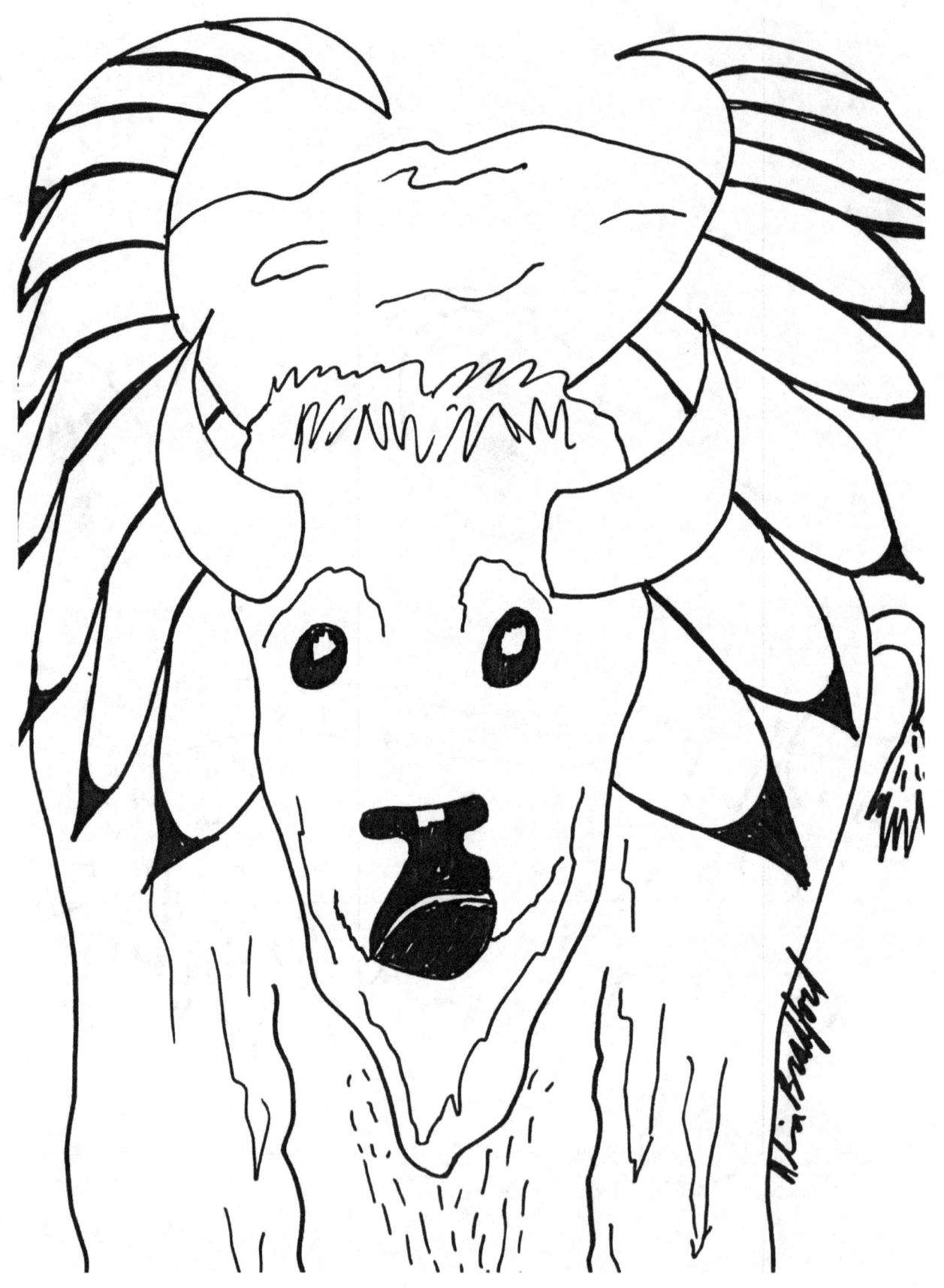

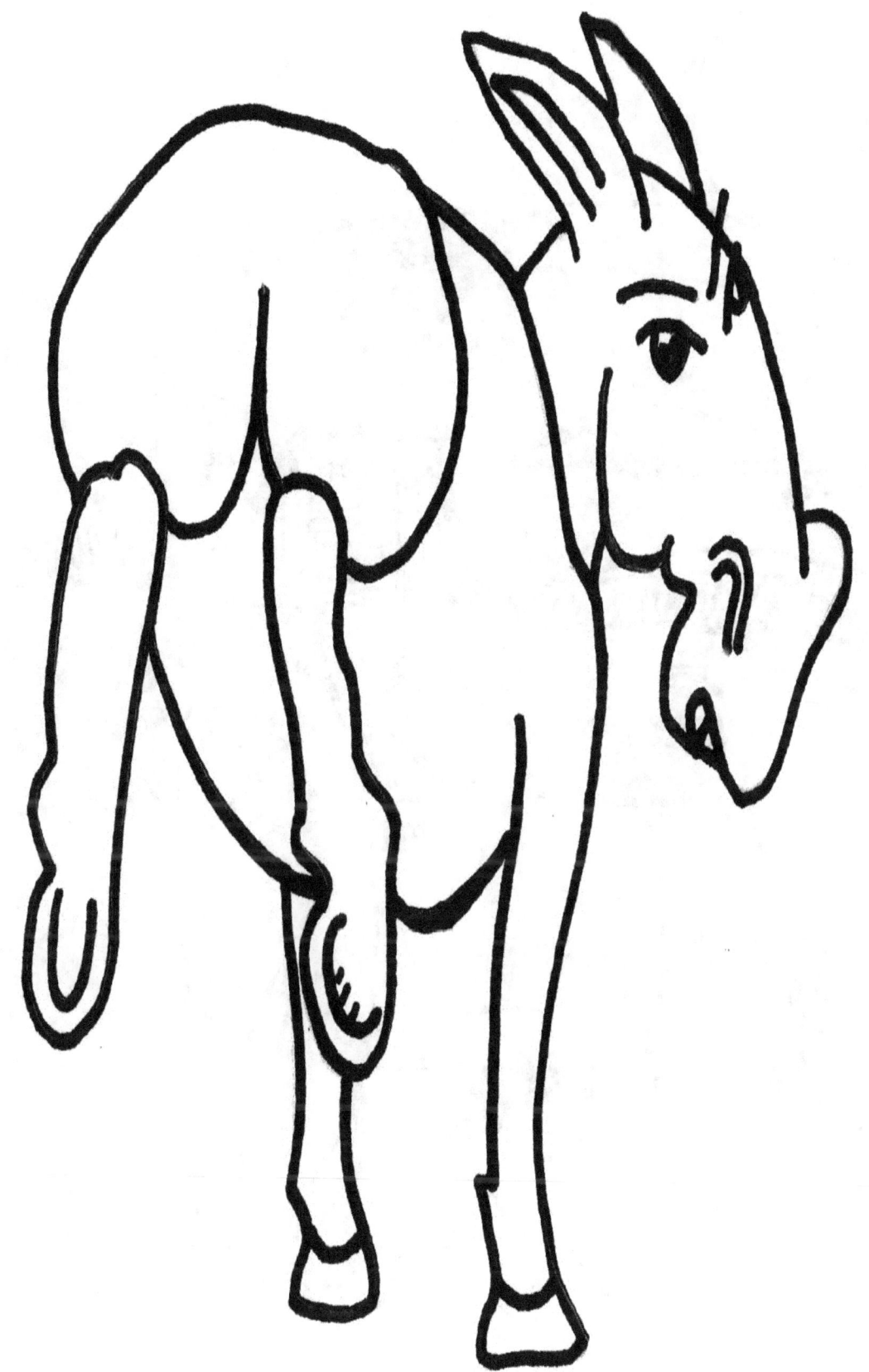

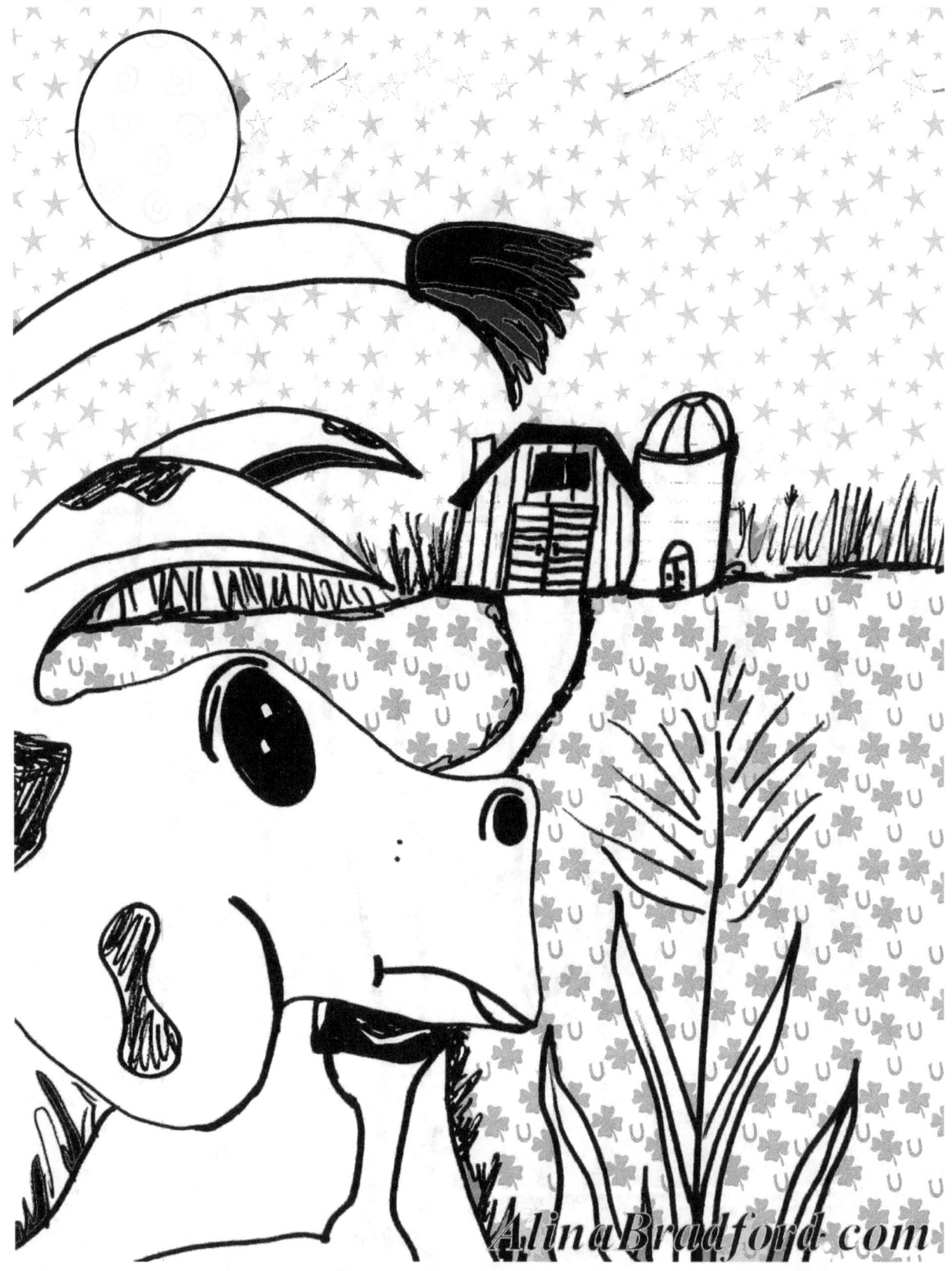

AlinaBradford.com

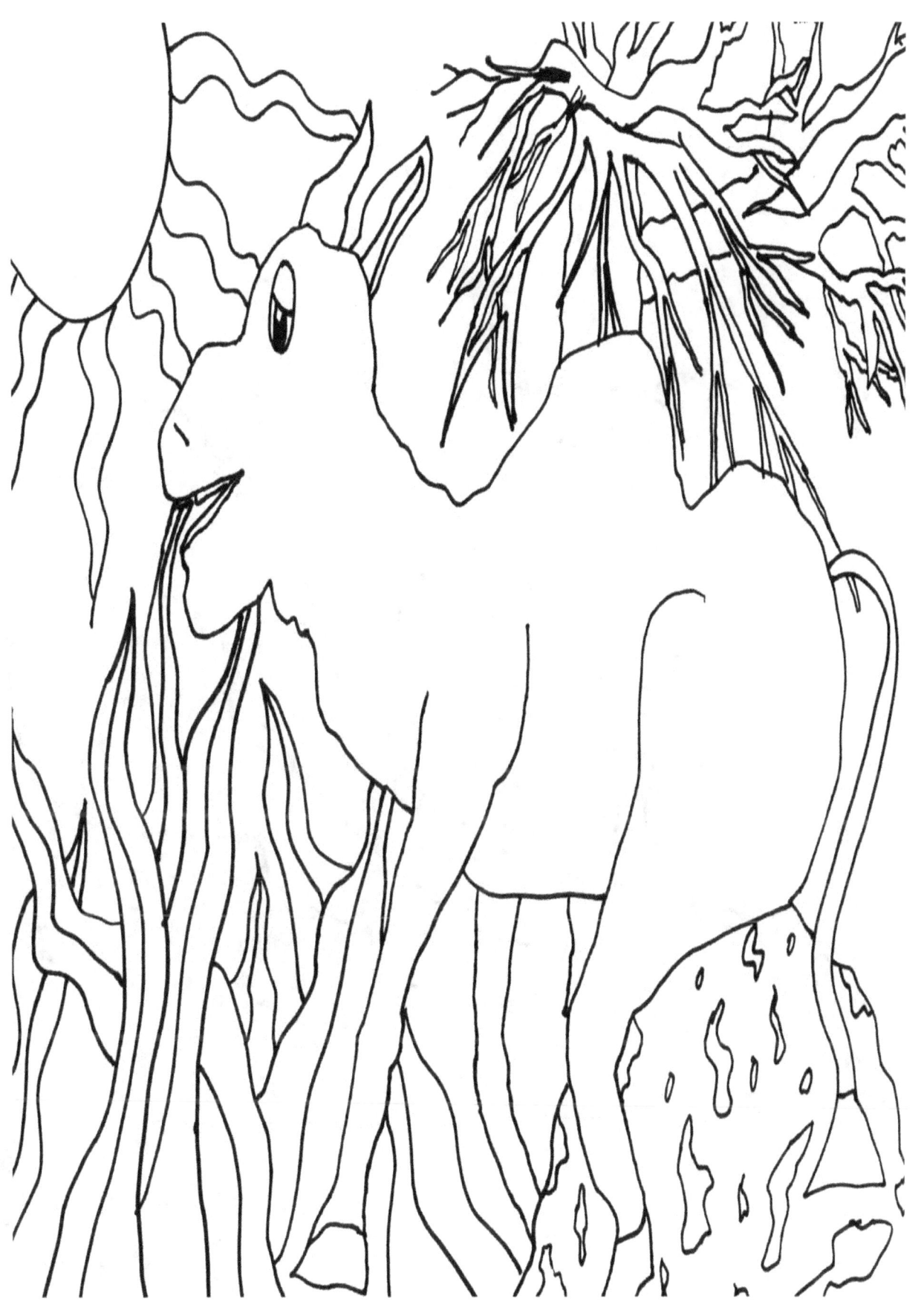

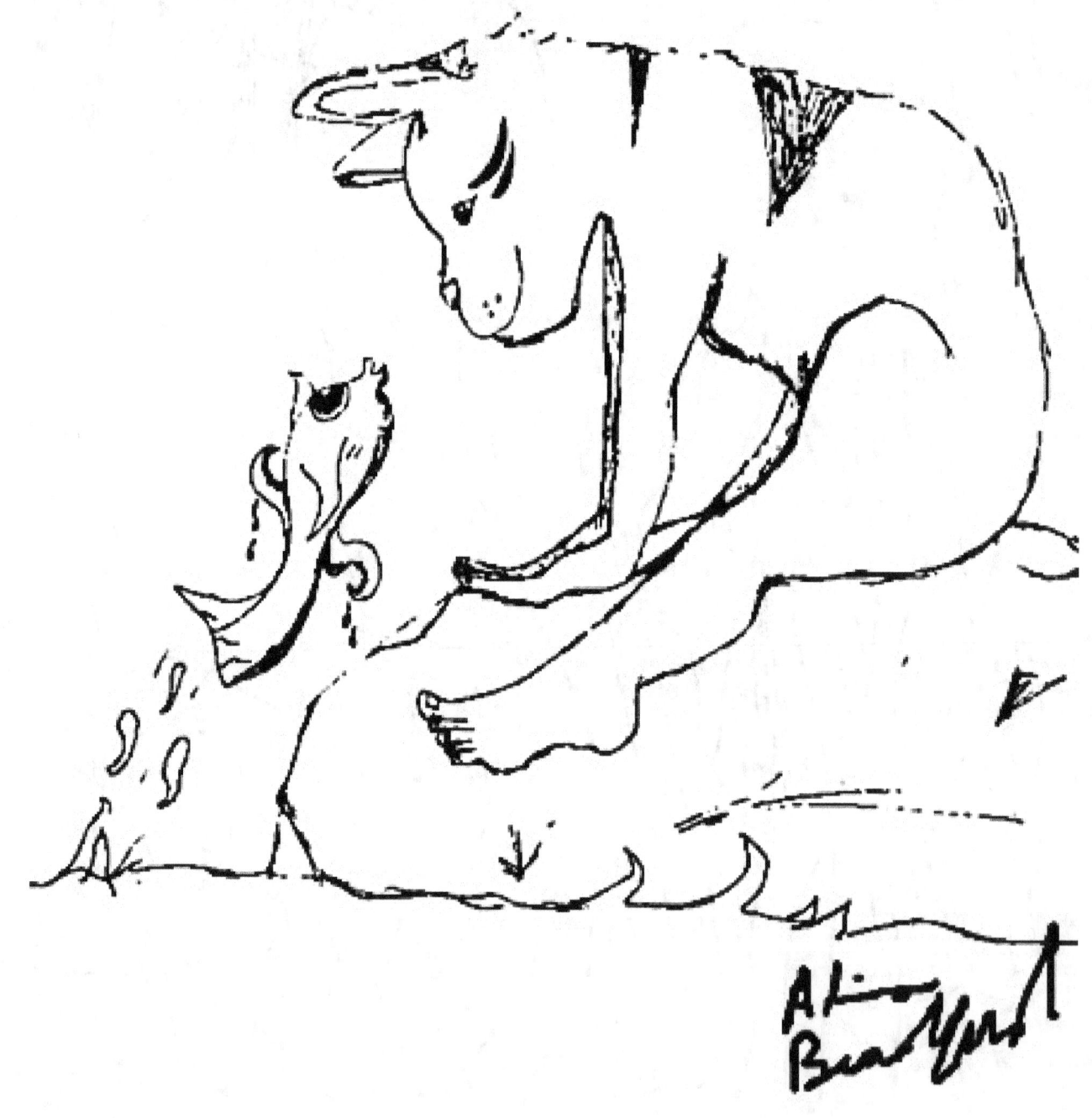

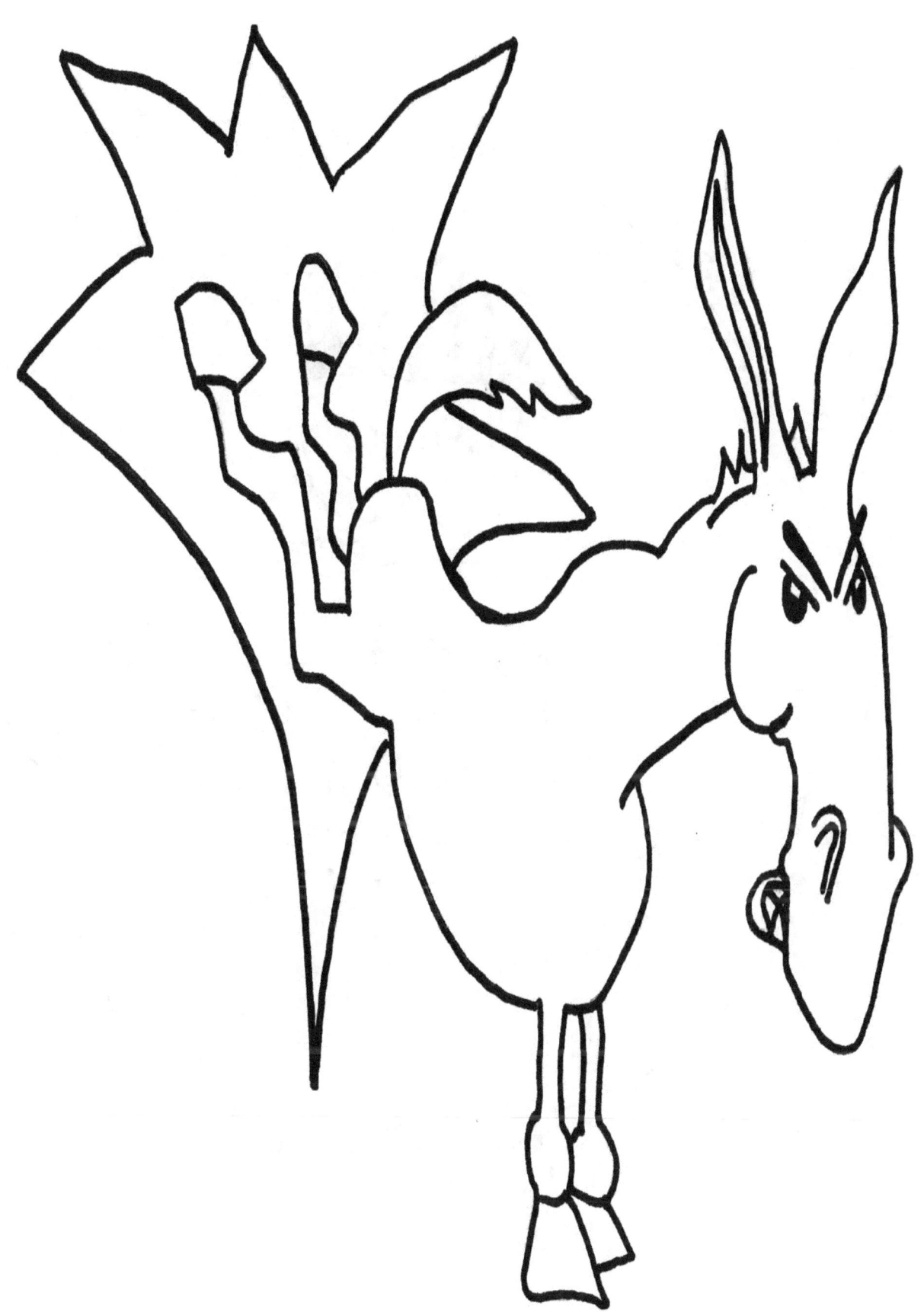

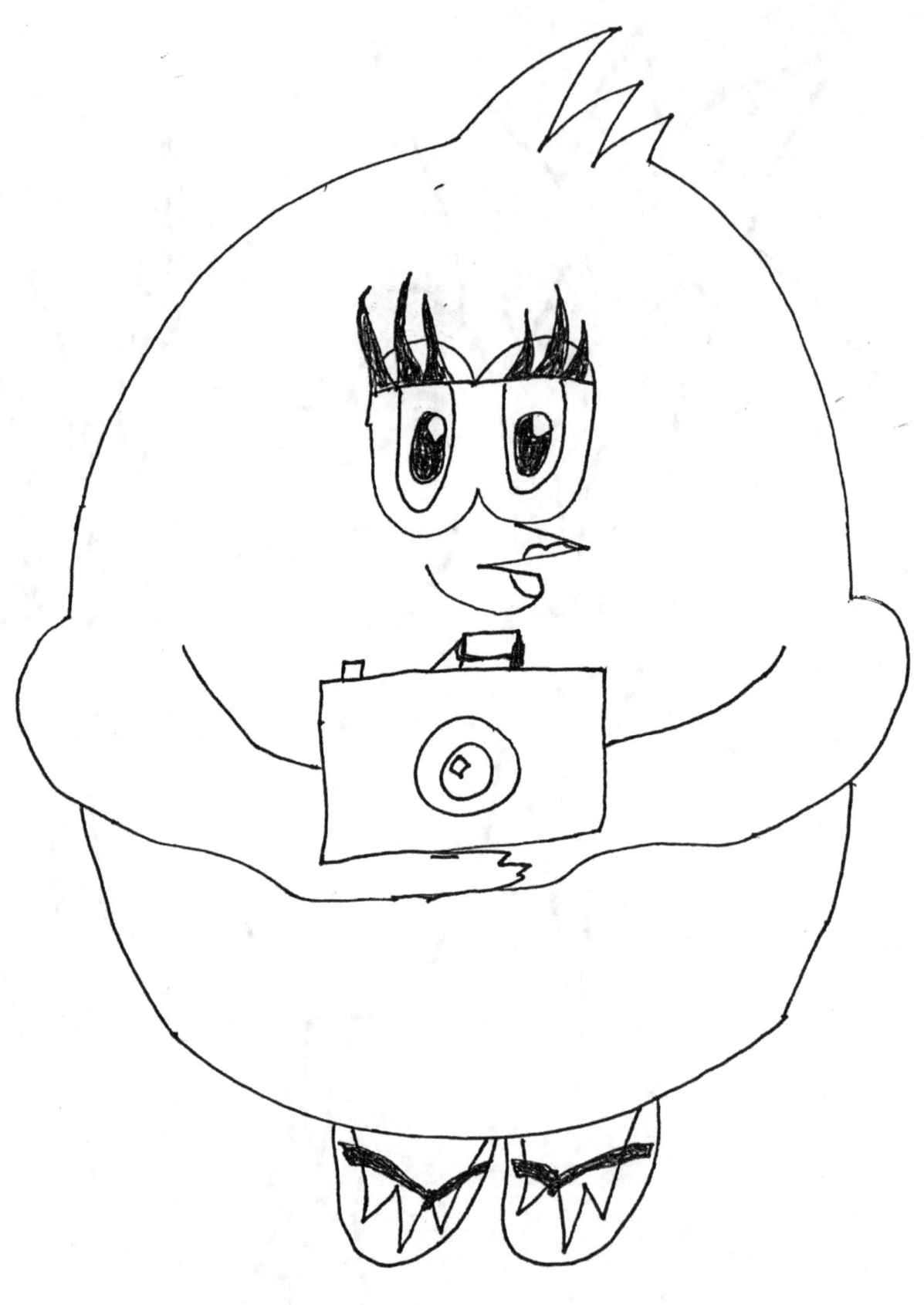

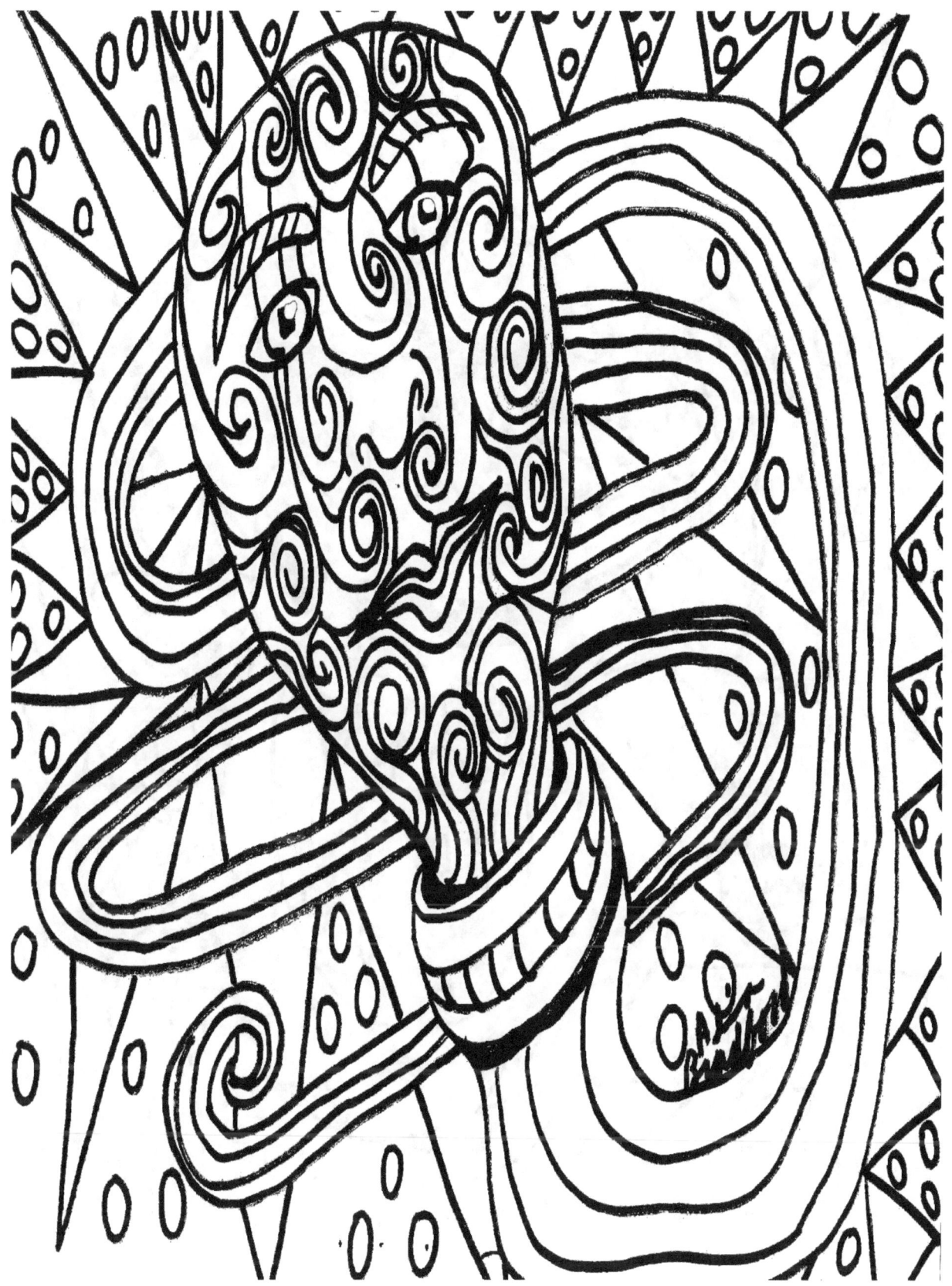

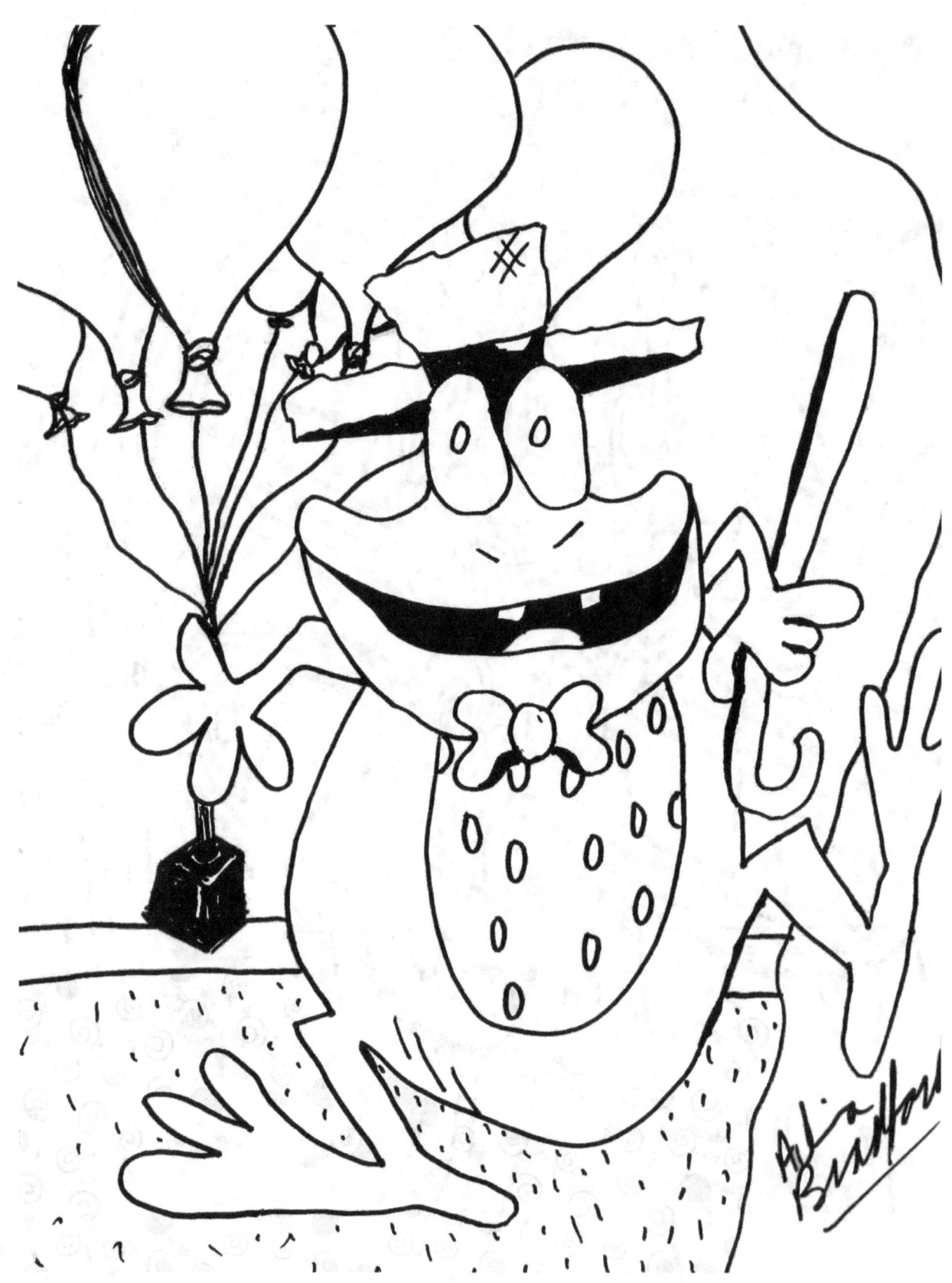

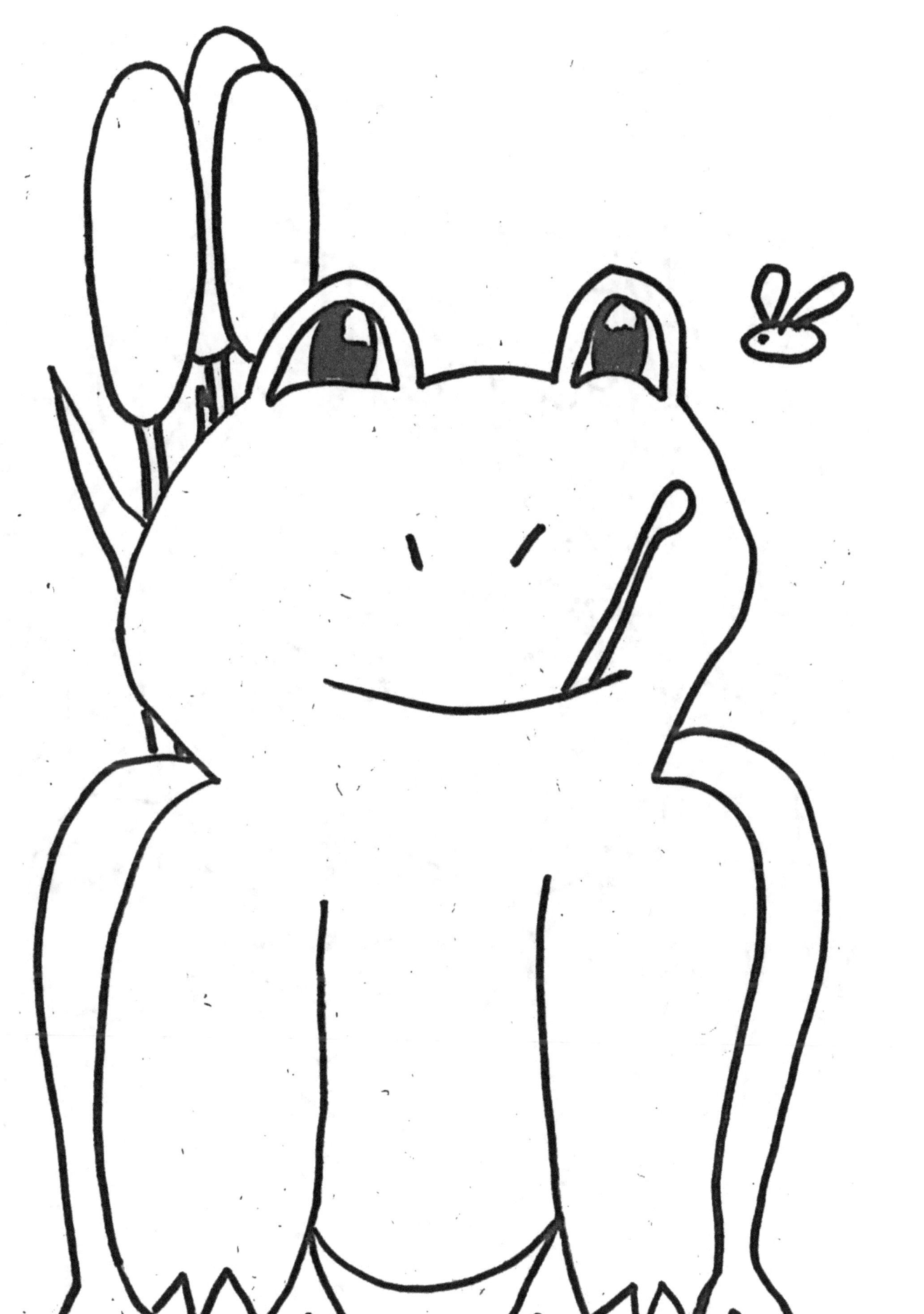

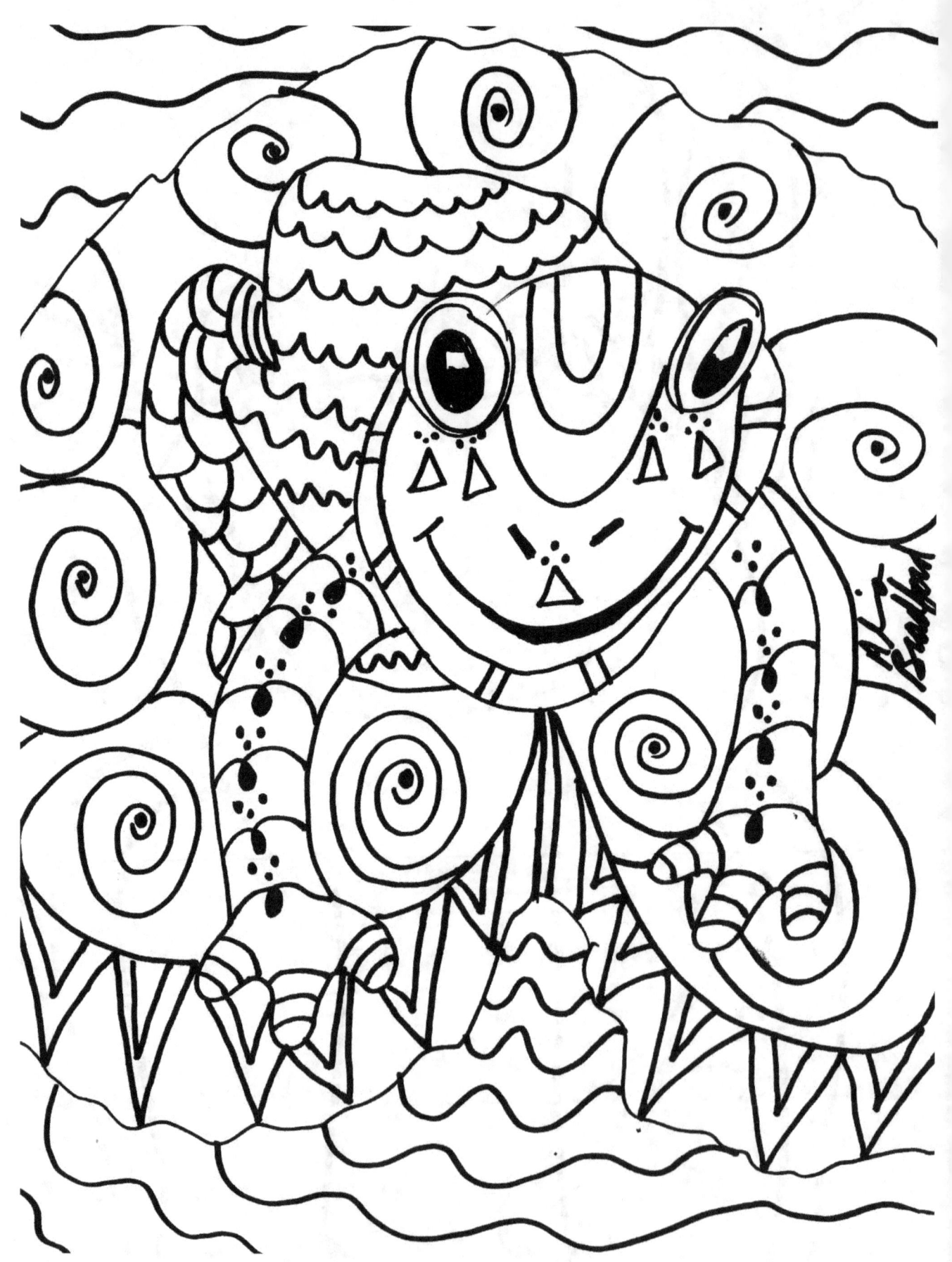

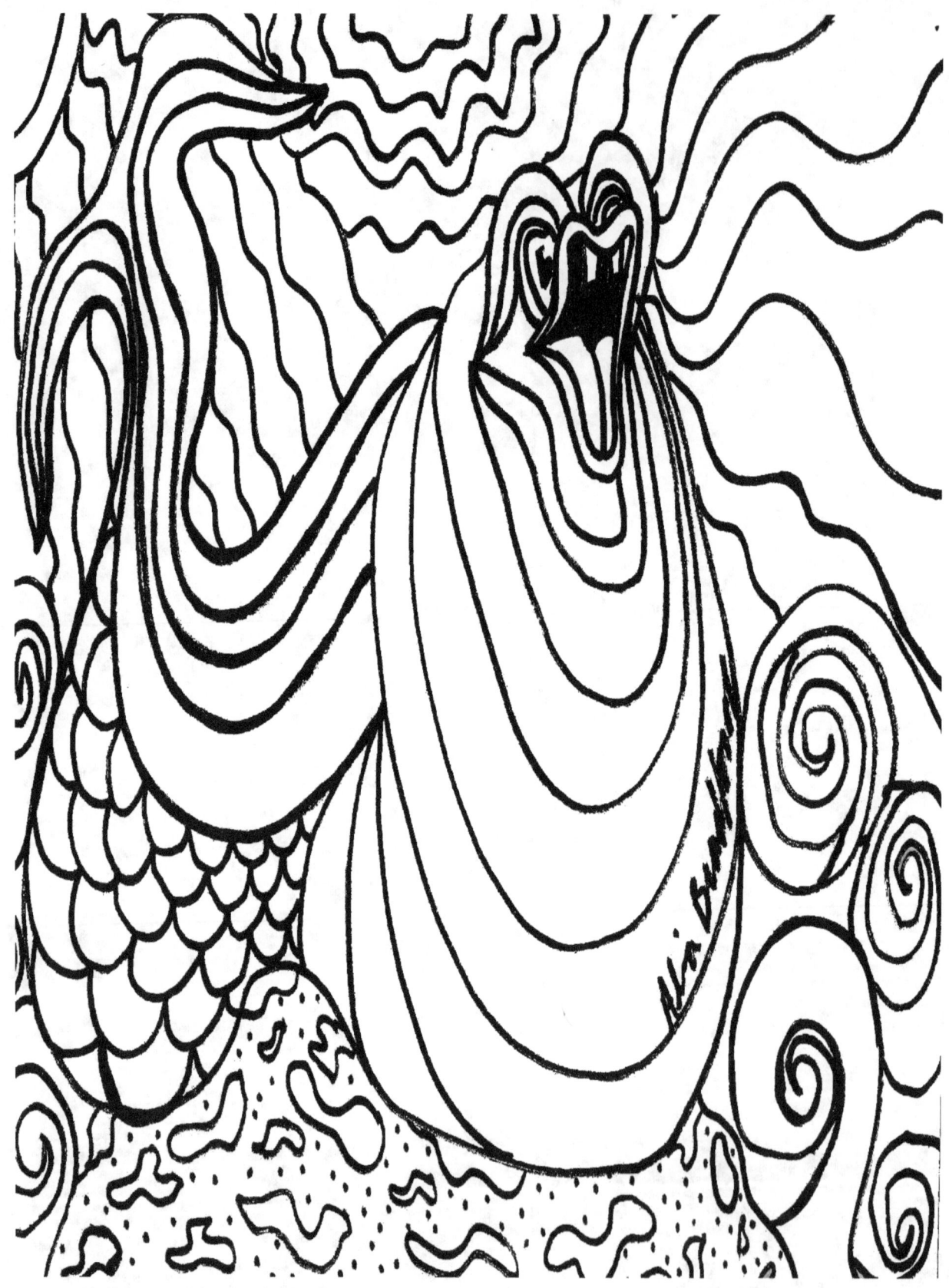

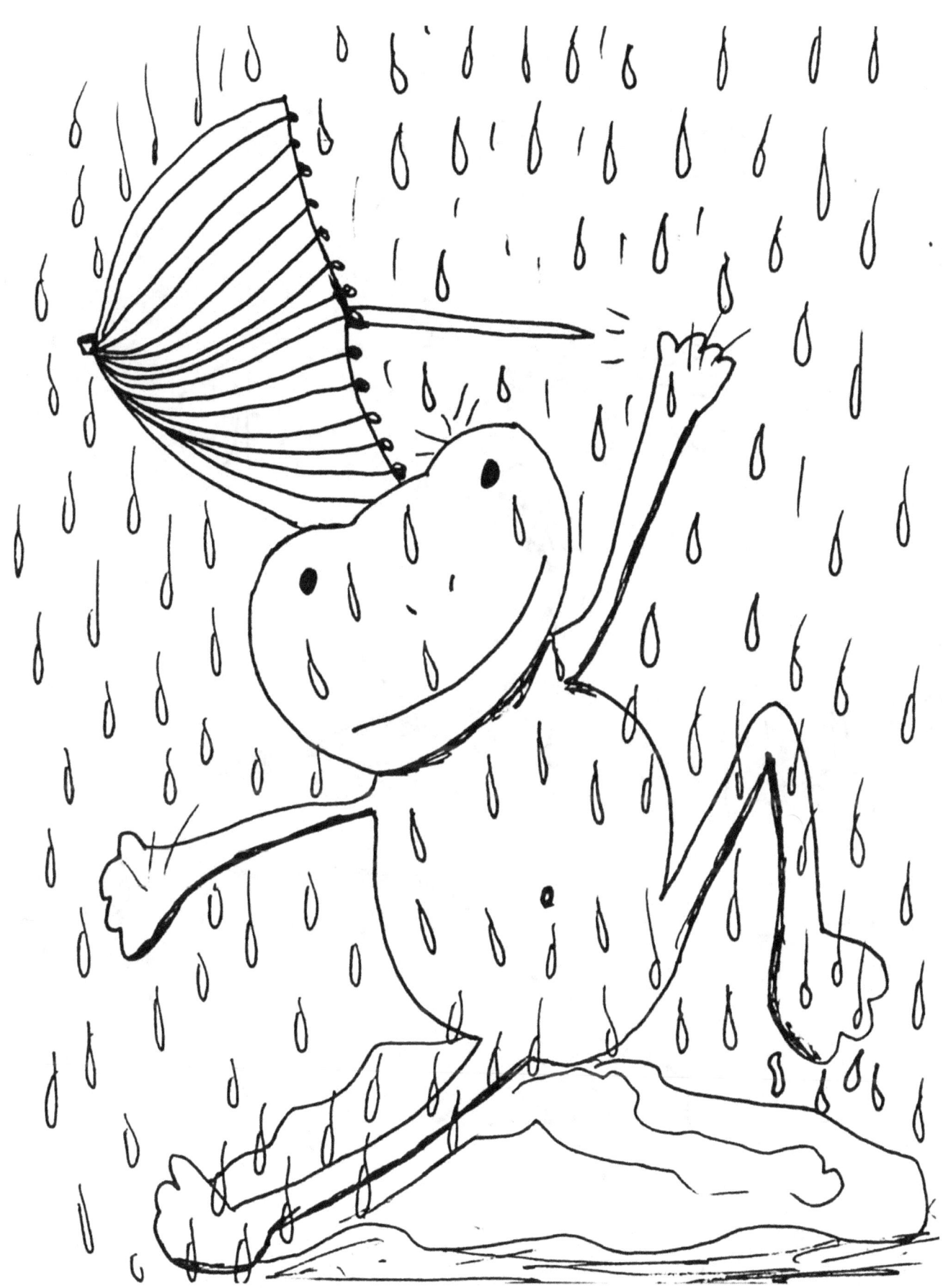

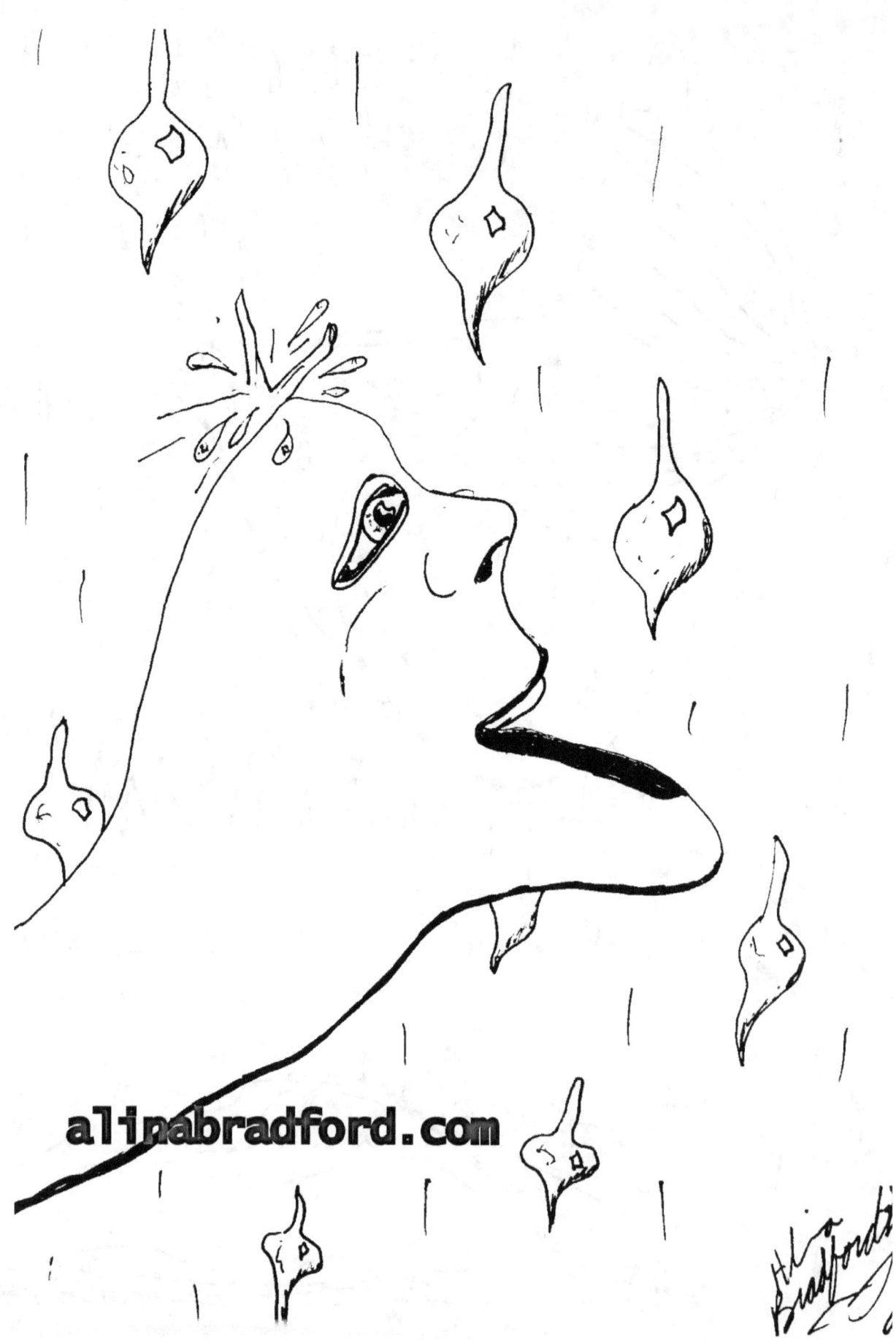

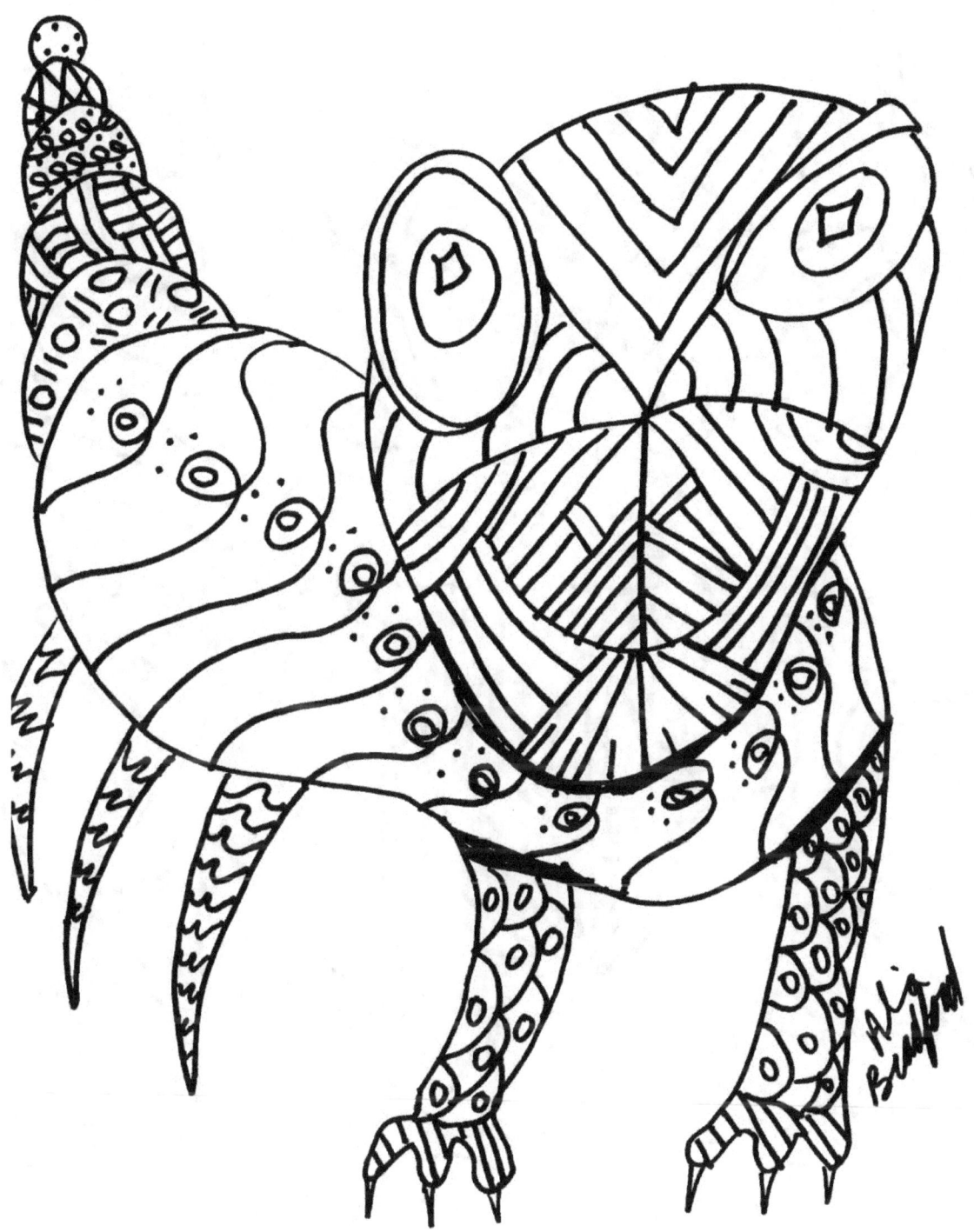

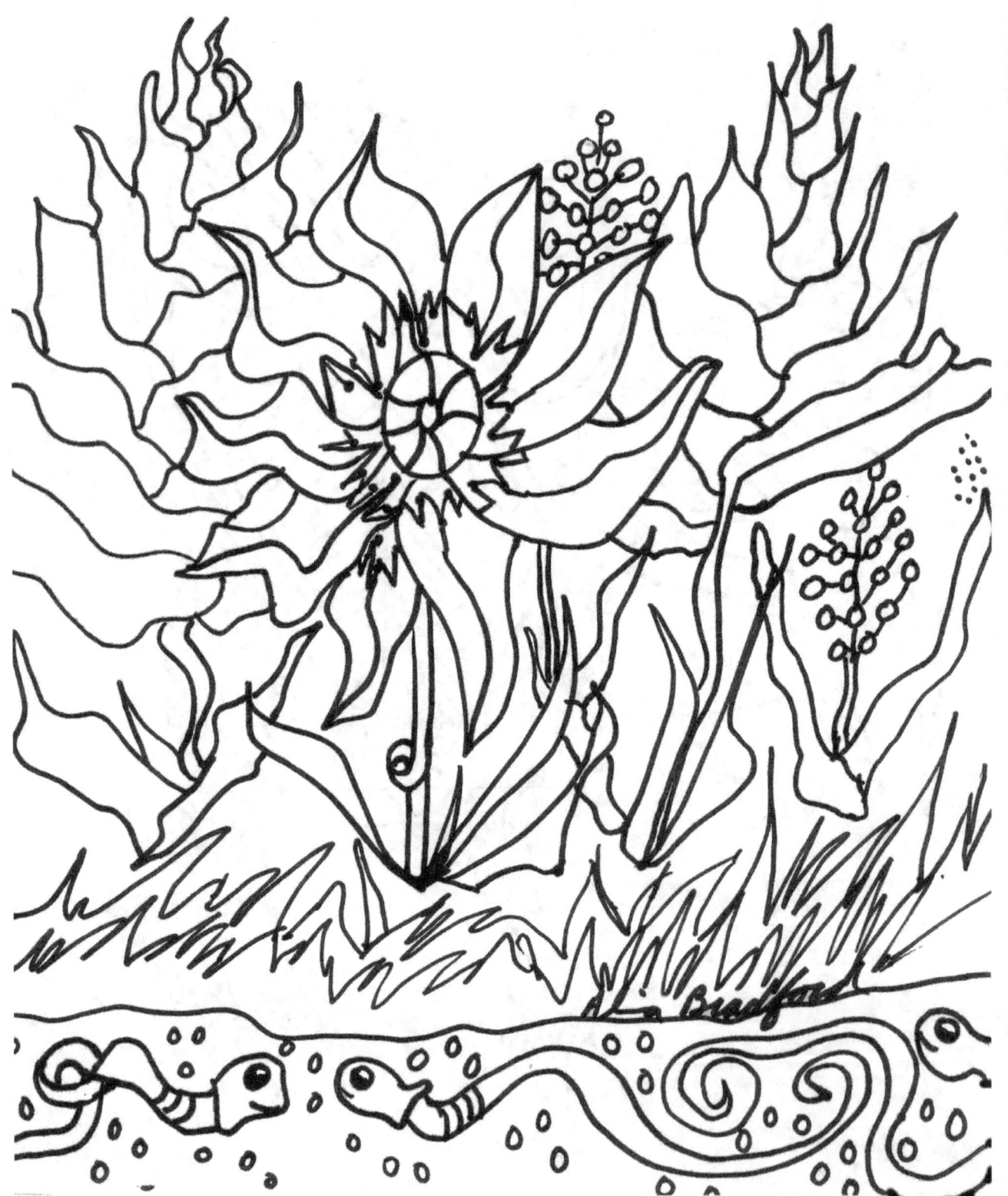

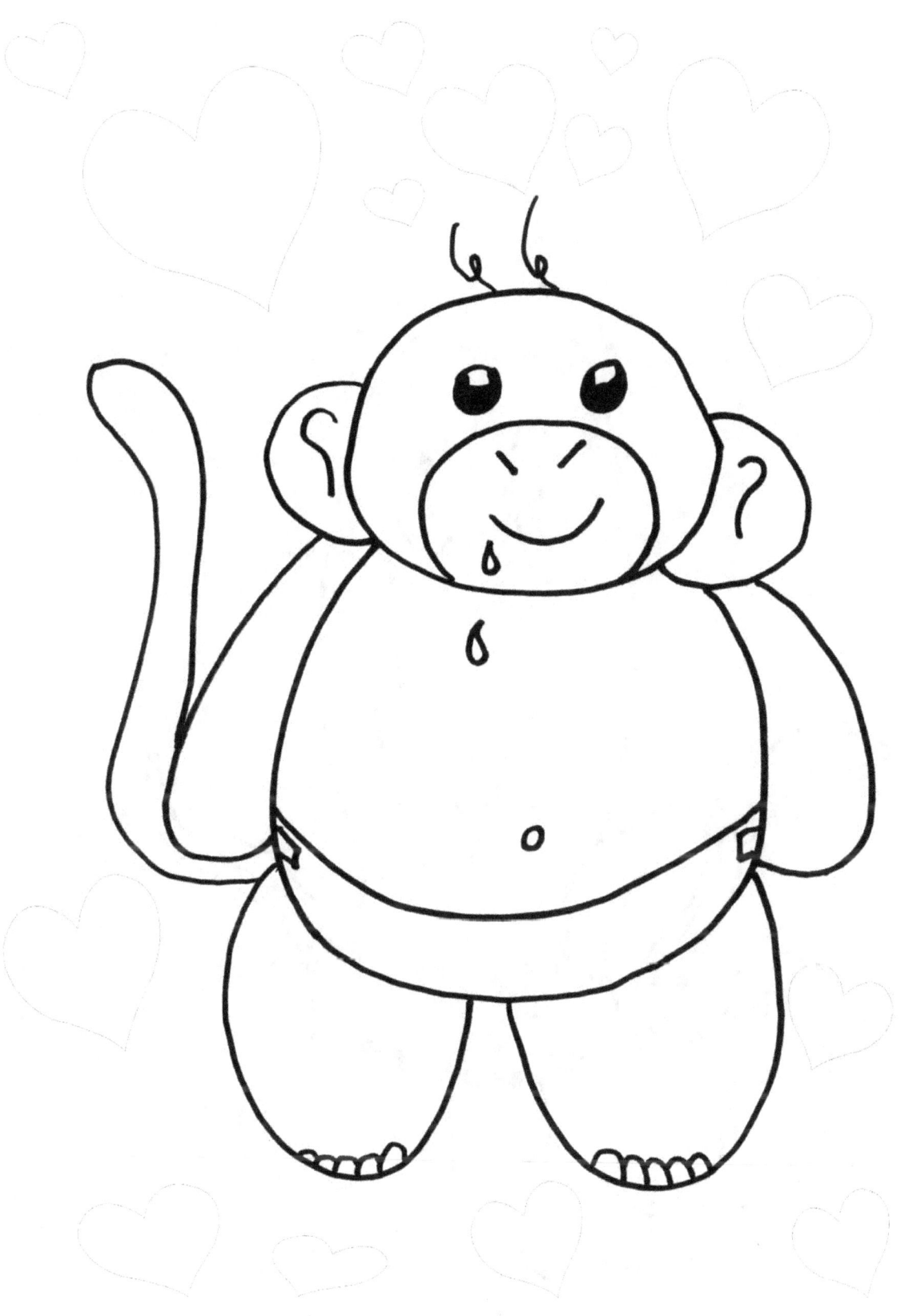

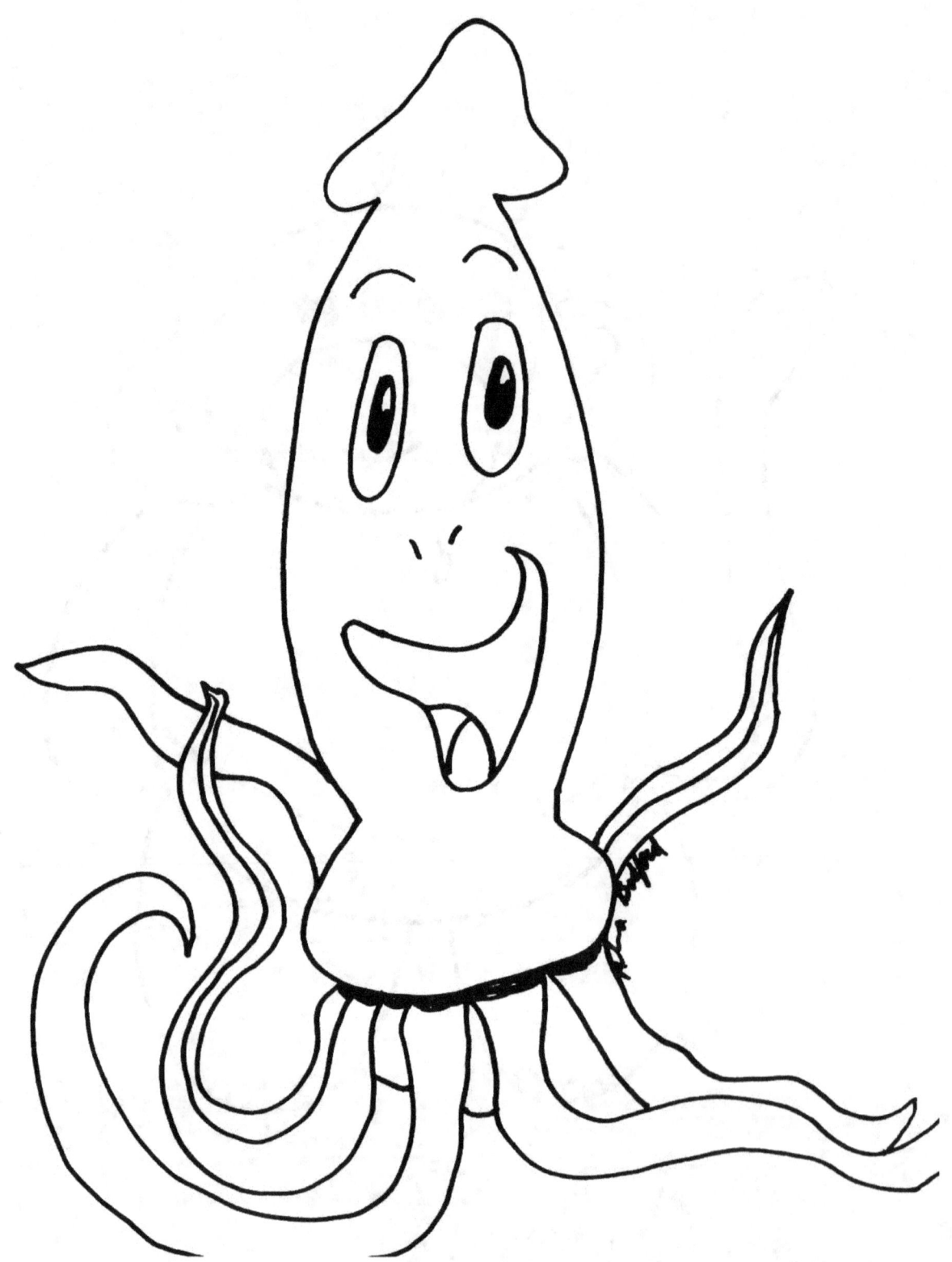

CROCHET CAT MAKES

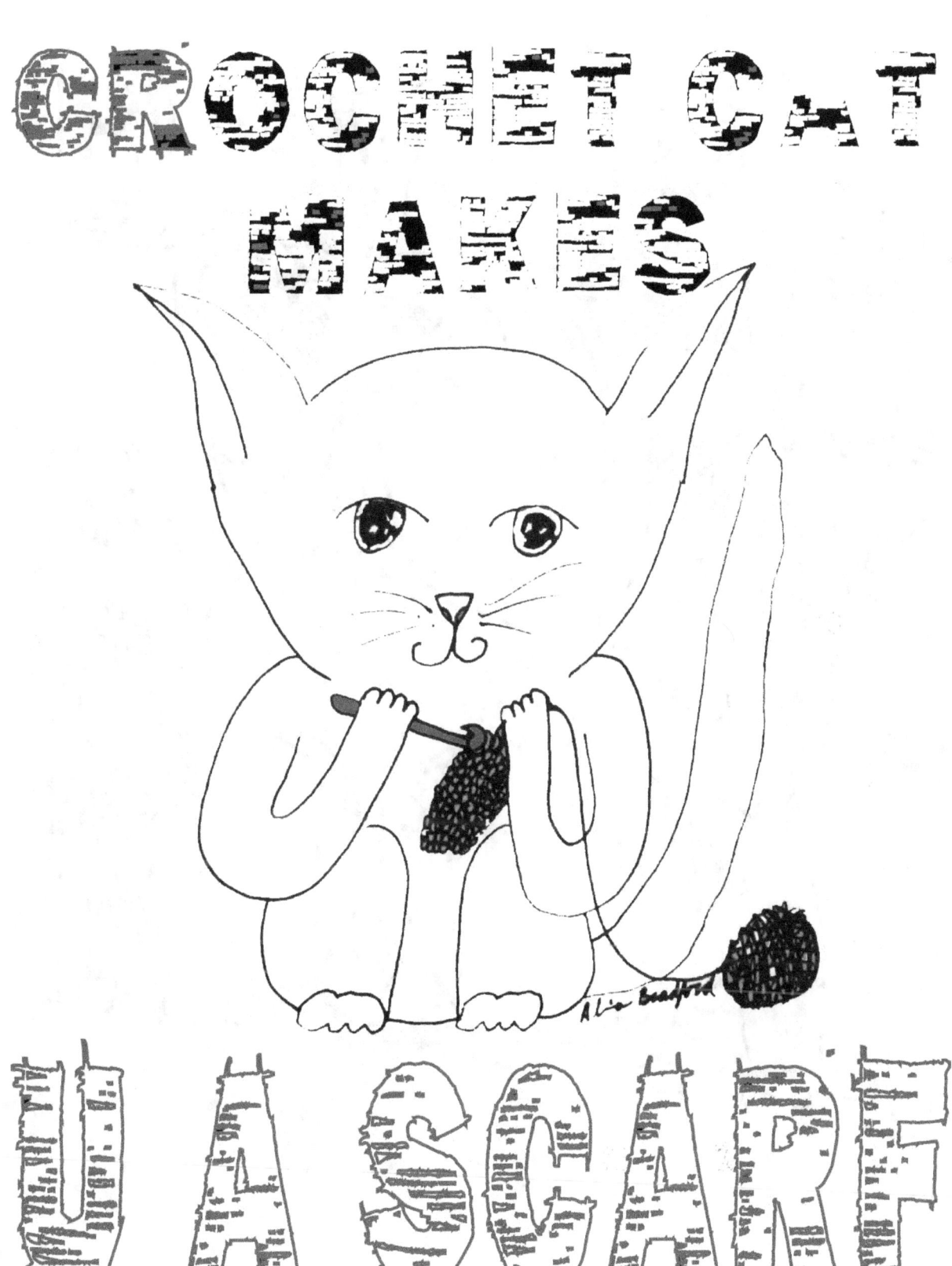

U A SCARF

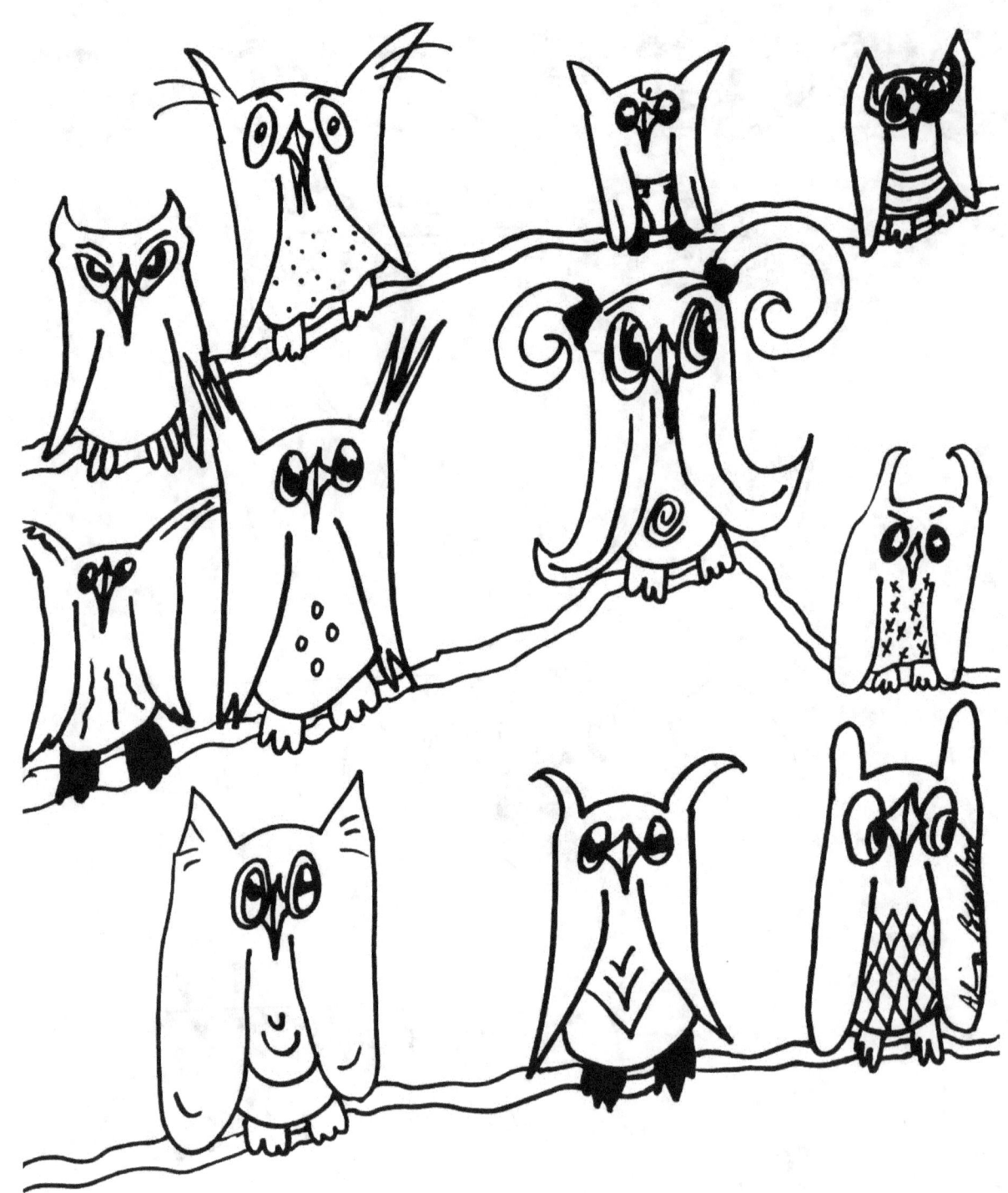

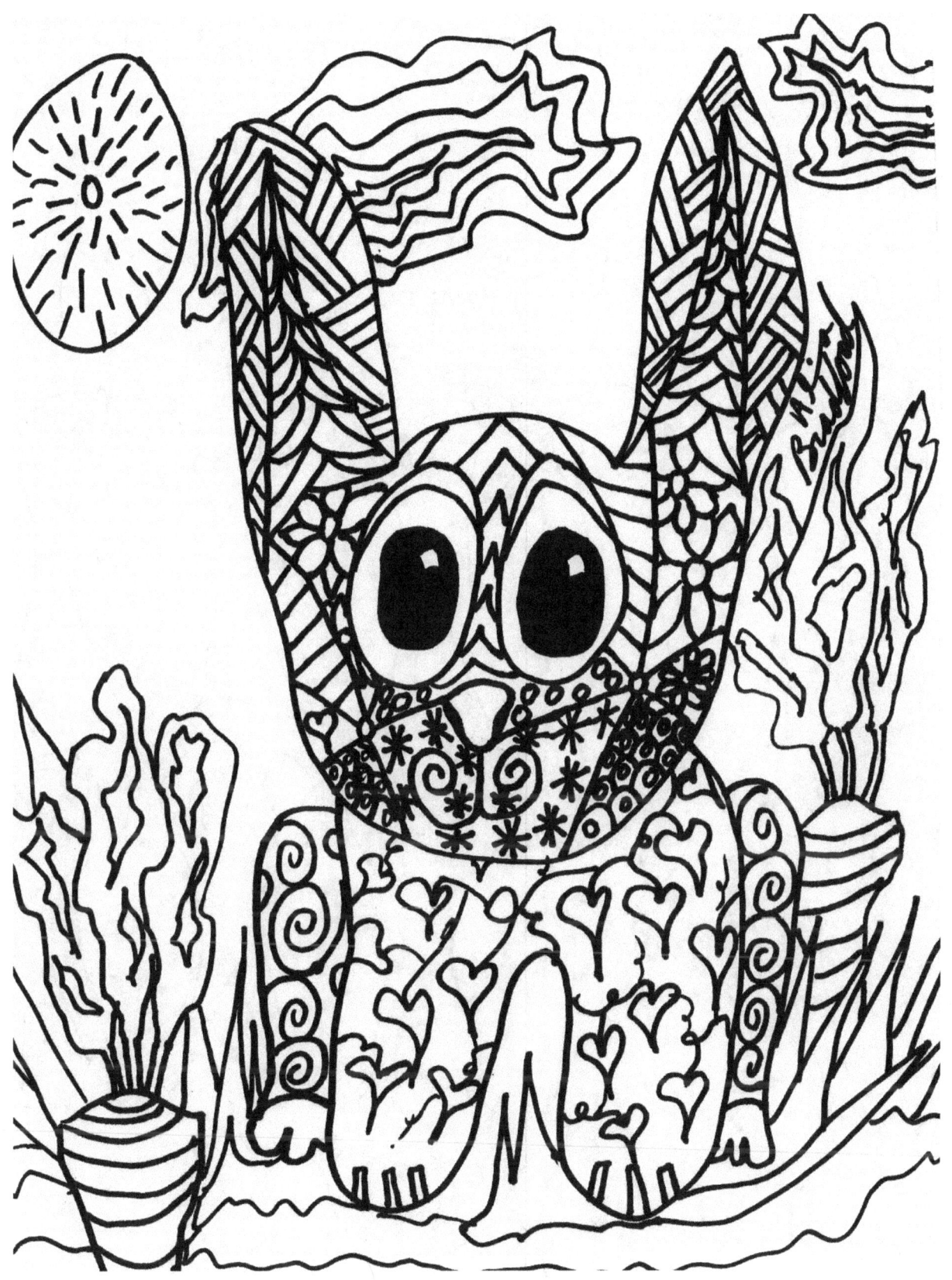

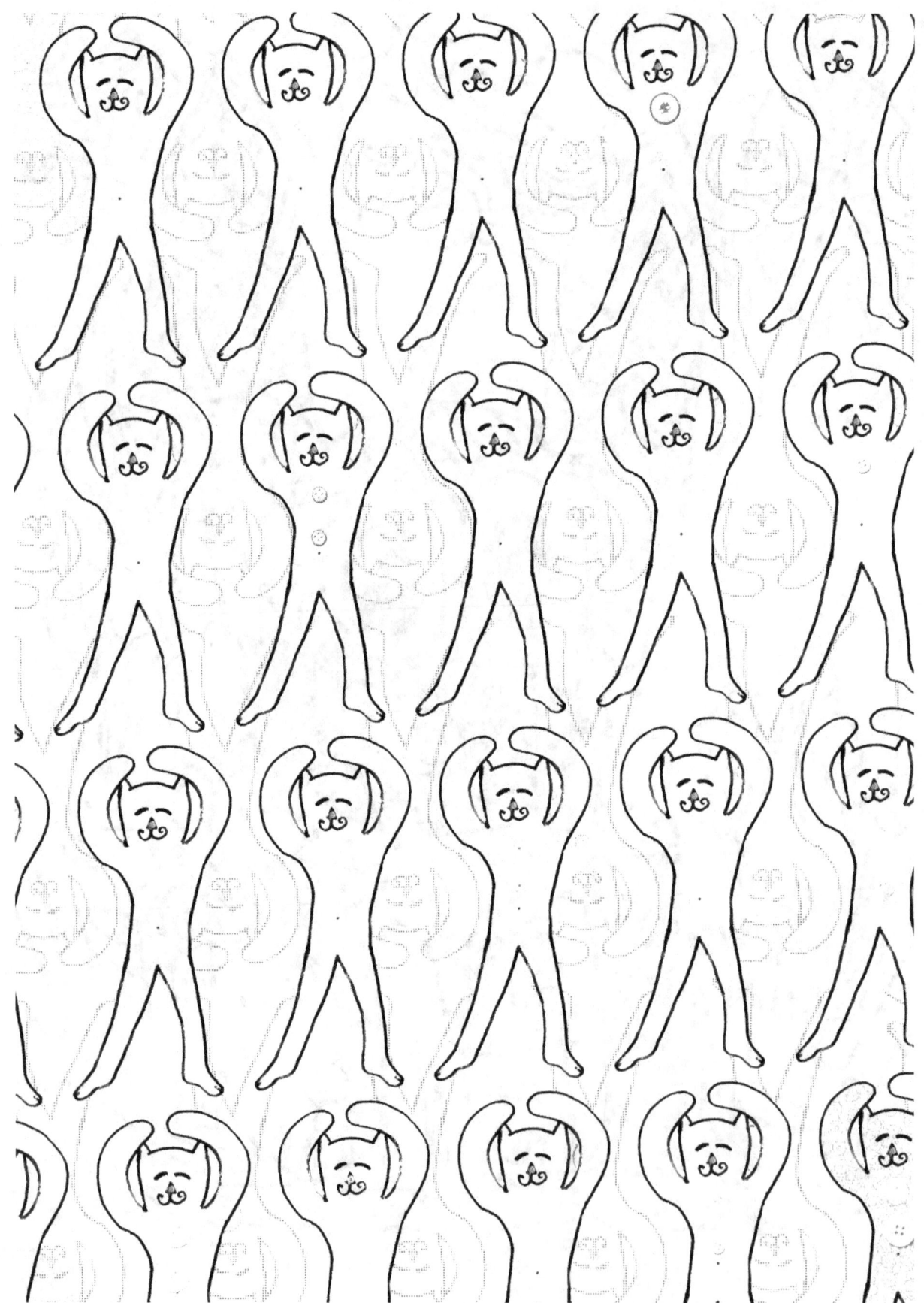

www.ingramcontent.com/pod-product-compliance
Lightning Source LLC
Chambersburg PA
CBHW081417170526
45166CB00010B/3379